food style

brunches

acknowledgements

Firstly, I would like to express my deepest thanks to Anne Wilson and Catie Ziller for the opportunity to write three more books and for having the clear publishing vision that I have been privileged to be a part of for the past four years. To Susan Gray, my patient and careful editor, for picking up all the "oopses". To Marylouise Brammer, the talented designer who has given time, love and dedication to making these books truly beautiful. To Ben Dearnley, the photographer, and Kristen Anderson, the food stylist, for blessing me with their professionalism, friendship but most of all talent for a very special six weeks—thank you for your generosity. To Anna Waddington, project manager and walking angel, for organizing me and my manicness. To Jane Lawson, the new torchbearer, for listening, laughing and yumming with me. To David, Bec, Kate, Lulu and Melita for sharing my passion for food and for making work a special place. To Ross Dobson and Michaela Le Compte for testing and tasting my recipes with me and sharing their knowledge. To Donna Hay, lady princess, gifted fellow foodie and friend, just for being who she is. To Mum, Matt, Relle, Rhearn, Nathan, Trace, Scottie, Paulie and Kim for their positive feedback, love and patience. To Penel, Michael, Shem and Gabe for a bond and sealant in the form of love that keeps me afloat. To Jude, for doing the yards with me with such honesty and caring. To Dundee for the pearls of wisdom. To Mel, Chaska, Rod, Pete, Fish, Olivia, Annie, Daz, Col, Richie, Melanie, Sean, Anne, George, Yvette, Woody, Ulla, Glenn, Boyd, Sal, Birdie and Dave for enjoying eating as much as I enjoy cooking. Thanks too to the Antico family for sourcing all the hard-to-find fruit and veggies I needed.

The publisher wishes to thank the following for their generosity in supplying props for the book: Anibou; Bison Homewares; Boda Nova; The Bay Tree; Country Road Homewear; David Jones; Domestic Pots—pieces by Lex Dickson, Simon Reece, Victor Greenaway, Helen Stephens; EQ-IQ; Funkis Swedish Forms; Culti; Empire Homeware; Ikea; Wild Rhino.

Front cover: pandoro with poached peaches and mascarpone, page 37.

food style

brunches

jody vassallo

TIME
LIFE
BOOKS

contents

Seasonal fresh fruit is a wonderfully quick accompaniment to brunch or can simply be served on its own…

halved sweet sugar bananas drenched with golden syrup or honey and finished with chopped macadamia nuts

fresh mixed berries standing alone

colorful fruit platter using mango, sliced guava, grapes, kiwi fruit and ripe baby pears

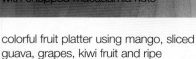

fresh passion fruit frozen in their shells

luscious red pomegranates drizzled with a combination of rose water and apple juice

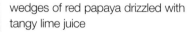

pyramids of pineapple and star fruit slices with maple syrup and shaved toasted coconut

wedges of red papaya drizzled with tangy lime juice

sweet figs and fresh dates with thick honey yogurt sprinkled with toasted pine nuts

Complete your brunch with an indulgent beverage or two …

fresh banana and ripe mango blended with vanilla soy milk and honey yogurt

vodka, tomato juice, a few drops of tobasco, worcestershire and celery salt

decadent caffe latte infused with a vanilla bean

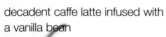

chilly iced chocolate

chilled fresh guava juice

espresso with a pinch of ground cinnamon and cinnamon sticks

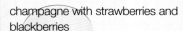

champagne with strawberries and blackberries

ginger ale and fresh pineapple juice punch with ginger, strawberries and mint leaves

The "blt"—a toasted sandwich with bacon, lettuce and tomato— is here given a tempting new twist.

mediterranean blt

4 small vine-ripened tomatoes, halved
1 head garlic, halved
1 tablespoon extra-virgin olive oil
sea or regular salt and cracked black pepper
1/4 cup basil leaves
1 loaf Italian bread
8 slices provolone cheese
8 slices mortadella
1 bunch arugula
extra-virgin olive oil, extra
balsamic vinegar

Preheat the oven to 400°F. Place the tomatoes and garlic in a roasting pan and drizzle with the oil. Sprinkle with sea salt and cracked black pepper and roast for 40 minutes or until the garlic is soft and the tomatoes are slightly dried. Add the basil leaves and continue baking for 5 minutes or until the leaves are crisp.
Remove from the oven.
Cut 4 thick slices from the loaf of bread and lightly toast on both sides. Peel the roasted garlic cloves and spread half onto the toast. Top with the provolone, mortadella, arugula, basil and roasted tomatoes. Sprinkle with the remaining roasted garlic, drizzle with olive oil and balsamic vinegar and serve immediately.

Serves 4

Haloumi is a firm, salty sheep's milk cheese with a rubbery texture. It is widely used in Greek cooking.

fried green tomatoes with haloumi

Place the haloumi, garlic, lemon juice, vinegar and olive oil in a nonmetallic dish and marinate for at least 3 hours. Drain well and reserve the marinade. Fry the haloumi in a nonstick frying pan over medium heat until golden brown on both sides. Remove and set aside. Add the cherry and teardrop tomatoes and cook until the skins burst. Remove and keep warm. Heat the marinade and add it to the cooked tomatoes. Dip the green tomato slices into the buttermilk, then coat in the cornmeal. Heat the oil in a large, nonstick frying pan and pan-fry the tomatoes over medium heat until brown. Drain on paper towels. Serve the haloumi on a bed of arugula topped with tomatoes and drizzled with the reserved marinade. Sprinkle with marjoram leaves.

Serves 4

1 lb haloumi, cut into 1/2-inch thick slices
2 cloves garlic, crushed
2 tablespoons lemon juice
1 tablespoon balsamic vinegar
3 tablespoons extra-virgin olive oil
8 oz cherry tomatoes
8 oz teardrop (pear) tomatoes, halved
4 green tomatoes, cut into thick slices
1/2 cup buttermilk
1 cup cornmeal
oil, for pan-frying
1 bunch arugula
2 teaspoons marjoram leaves, to garnish

This frittata makes a wonderful brunch. Garnish and serve as the camembert melts onto the frittata.

salmon, dill and camembert frittata

12 eggs
1/2 cup grated parmesan
11/2 cups whipping cream
6 scallions, sliced
61/2 oz smoked salmon
1/4 cup chopped fresh dill
31/2 oz camembert, sliced
zest of 1 lemon
dill sprigs, to garnish

Preheat the oven to 350°F. Lightly grease and line a 9-inch springform pan. Make sure it is properly sealed, otherwise the filling will leak out. Lightly beat the eggs, parmesan and cream and stir in the scallions. Thinly slice 5 oz of the smoked salmon and add it to the egg mixture. Add the dill. Pour the mixture into the springform pan and place on a baking sheet. Bake for 50–60 minutes or until the frittata has set.
Allow to cool slightly before removing from the pan. Arrange the remaining smoked salmon and all of the sliced camembert decoratively in the center of the frittata. Garnish with lemon zest and dill sprigs and serve immediately.

Serves 6–8

corn fritters with crispy prosciutto

Preheat the oven to 400°F. Place the tomatoes on a nonstick baking sheet, sprinkle with salt and pepper and bake for 30 minutes or until tender. Chop and combine with the chutney.

Sift the flour, cornmeal and sugar into a large bowl and whisk in the combined egg and buttermilk until smooth. Fold in the corn, scallions, chives and parmesan. Add salt and pepper to taste. Heat the oil in a nonstick frying pan and spoon 3 tablespoons of the corn mixture into the pan. Cook for 2 minutes over a medium heat, or until bubbles burst on the surface. Turn over and cook until golden. Continue cooking fritters until all the mixture is used up. Keep the cooked fritters warm. Broil the prosciutto until crisp. Serve stacks of fritters drizzled with tomato chutney and topped with prosciutto and chervil leaves.

Serves 4

NOTE: Corn mixture may be made ahead of time and kept covered in the refrigerator. Add extra liquid if the mixture thickens.

8 ripe plum tomatoes, halved
sea or regular salt and freshly ground
    black pepper
1/2 cup spicy tomato chutney
11/2 cups self-rising flour
1/2 cup coarse cornmeal
1 teaspoon sugar
1 egg, lightly beaten
11/2 cups buttermilk
2 cobs corn, kernels removed, or
    2 cups corn kernels, drained
4 scallions, chopped
2 tablespoons fresh snipped chives
1/4 cup grated parmesan
4 tablespoons olive oil
12 thin slices prosciutto
chervil leaves, to garnish

"Mandarin" was the name given
by the British to a loose-skinned
citrus fruit imported from China.

tangy mandarin lime granita

1 cup superfine sugar
1/2 cup water
1 teaspoon finely chopped
mandarin zest
1 teaspoon finely chopped lime zest
2 cups mandarin juice

Place the sugar and water in a saucepan and stir over low heat until the sugar dissolves. Bring to a boil and cook over high heat for 5 minutes or until syrupy. Remove from heat and add the mandarin and lime zest and the mandarin juice.

Transfer the syrup to a shallow metal pan, cover with foil and place in the freezer for 1 hour or until the edges begin to freeze. Scrape with a fork to break up the ice crystals, cover and return to the freezer. Repeat 4 times at 50-minute intervals, then allow to freeze completely. Use a fork to scrape the granita into large shavings and serve immediately in small bowls.

Serves 4

Jarlsberg hails from Norway and is a delicately flavored, holey cheese with a lovely buttery color.

smoky ham, egg and jarlsberg cheese sandwiches

Spread 8 slices of bread with the dijon mustard.
Heat the oil in a nonstick frying pan, add the eggs and fry until cooked to your liking (soft in the center works best). Top 4 of the slices of bread with some shaved ham, an egg and the cheese, then a slice of bread on top. Butter the outside of each sandwich, top and bottom. Heat a frying pan over medium heat and cook the sandwiches in batches, with a plate on top of them to weigh them down, until crisp and golden on both sides. You will know they are ready when the cheese starts melting and oozing out of the sides. Serve immediately.

Serves 4

NOTE: These also work well when made in a toasted sandwich maker.

1 unsliced loaf white bread, cut into 3/4-inch thick slices
3 tablespoons dijon mustard
1 tablespoon vegetable oil
4 eggs
10 oz shaved or finely sliced honey-smoked ham
5 oz shaved jarlsberg or swiss cheese
2 tablespoons butter, softened

Before forming into balls, the
yogurt needs 4 days to drain in
cheesecloth to remove any liquid.

maple yogurt balls with sugary balsamic pears

2 lb thick, natural yogurt
1/2 cup maple syrup
square of cheesecloth
1 tablespoon ground cinnamon
2 tablespoons superfine sugar
1 1/2 cups hazelnuts, toasted
and roughly chopped
2/3 cup butter
1/2 cup brown sugar
1/4 cup balsamic vinegar
3 small bosc pears, sliced lengthwise

Combine the yogurt and maple syrup,
place onto a large square of doubled
cheesecloth, gather the cheesecloth
together and tie tightly together with
string. Loop the string around a
chopstick and suspend over a bowl
in the refrigerator for 4 days to drain
off any liquid.
Form 1 tablespoon of the mixture into a
ball with moistened hands and roll in a
cinnamon–sugar mixture. Then toss to
coat in the chopped hazelnuts. Repeat
with the remaining mixture.
Heat the butter in a large frying pan,
add the sugar and stir over low heat
until it dissolves. Stir in the balsamic
vinegar and bring the mixture to
a boil. Add the pears and simmer until
browned on both sides and slightly
soft. Arrange on serving plates and
top with the yogurt balls.

Serves 4

Frenching is the technique of
scraping meat away from the bone.
Ask your butcher to do this for you.

lamb cutlets with creamy spinach

Trim the lamb cutlets of any excess fat
or sinew and lightly coat each cutlet
in a little cracked black pepper.
Heat the oil in a frying pan and cook
the cutlets in batches over high heat for
3 minutes on each side or until cooked
to your liking. Remove from the pan
and keep warm.
Melt the butter in the frying pan and
add the garlic, scallions and spinach.
Cook until the scallions are soft and the
spinach wilts, then add the basil, cream
and mustard and cook until heated
through.
Serve the creamy spinach topped
with the peppered lamb cutlets and
warm roasted tomatoes.

Serves 4

8 frenched lamb cutlets
fresh cracked black pepper
1 tablespoon olive oil
2 tablespoons butter
2 cloves garlic, crushed
4 scallions, sliced
3/4 lb young spinach leaves, roughly
    chopped
1 tablespoon shredded fresh basil
1/4 cup whipping cream
2 tablespoons whole grain mustard
4 tomatoes, cut in half and roasted

Any small, spicy, precooked sausage could be used in this recipe e.g. chorizo, frankfurters or Italian sausages.

sweet potato and bell pepper rosti with spicy sausages

2 red bell peppers
1 lb waxy potatoes, unpeeled
11 oz sweet potatoes, peeled
1 onion, peeled and grated
2 tablespoons chopped fresh
cilantro leaves
3 tablespoons olive oil
8 chipolatas or any other small,
spicy, precooked sausages
1 bunch arugula
3 1/2 oz feta

Broil the bell peppers on high heat until the skins blister. Place in a plastic bag and allow to cool. Peel and cut into strips. Boil or steam the potatoes and sweet potatoes until tender. Allow to cool slightly, then peel and grate into a bowl. Add the onion, bell pepper and cilantro. Heat half of the oil in a large, nonstick frying pan, spread the mixture evenly over the bottom of the pan and cook over medium heat for 10 minutes or until the bottom is crisp and golden. Slide the rosti onto a plate, add the remaining oil to the pan, then flip the rosti back into the pan and cook for another 8 minutes. Remove and keep warm. Fry or broil the sausages until tender, then cut into thick slices. Cut the rosti into wedges and serve topped with arugula, sausage slices and crumbled feta.

Serves 4–6

Pistachio nuts are available all year round—if the shells are closed it means they are not ready to eat.

choc-chip and pistachio muffins

Preheat the oven to 400°F. Grease and line 10 1/2-cup muffin cups. Place the pistachios on a baking sheet and roast for 5 minutes. Remove from the oven and allow to cool. Place the pistachios and flour in a food processor and process until finely ground. Place the butter and confectioners' sugar in a bowl and beat until light and creamy. Sift together the pistachios and flour with the cocoa and cardamom and fold into the creamed mixture. Stir the egg whites into the creamed mixture, together with the chocolate chips, and mix to combine. Spoon the mixture into the prepared cups and bake for 25–30 minutes or until the muffins come away from the sides of the cups. Cool on wire racks. Dust lightly with confectioners' sugar.

Makes 10

1 cup shelled pistachio nuts
1/2 cup all-purpose flour
3/4 cup unsalted butter
12/3 cups confectioners' sugar
2 tablespoons cocoa
1/2 teaspoon ground cardamom
5 egg whites, lightly whisked
11/3 cups chocolate chips
confectioners' sugar, to serve

When Mr and Mrs Legrand Benedict
tired of eating the same old brunch,
Delmonicos in Manhattan made this.

eggs benedict

Hollandaise sauce
3/4 cup butter
4 egg yolks
2 tablespoons water
1 teaspoon tarragon vinegar

4 thick slices rye bread
8 slices ham
1 tablespoon vinegar
8 eggs

To make the hollandaise sauce, melt
the butter in a small saucepan and
transfer to a bowl. Place the egg yolks,
water and vinegar in a food processor
and, with the motor running, gradually
add the butter. Process until thick
and creamy.

Toast the bread on both sides and
top with the ham slices.

Half-fill a deep frying pan with water,
bring to a slow simmer and add the
vinegar. One by one, break the eggs
onto a plate and slide them into the
pan. Cook for 3 minutes or until done
to your liking.

Top each piece of toast and ham
with two poached eggs, and drizzle
with the hollandaise sauce.

Serves 4

Lemongrass is an herb with a subtle citrus flavor. It complements both sweet and savory dishes.

lemongrass creamed rice

Rinse the rice in a colander until the water runs clear. Drain well. Place the milk in a saucepan, add the lemongrass, sugar and vanilla and heat until the liquid is nearly boiling. Add the rice and stir for 1 minute or until the liquid returns to a boil. Reduce the heat and allow to simmer for 1 hour, stirring occasionally or until the rice is tender. Remove and discard the lemongrass. Divide the rice among 4 bowls and top with the sliced fruit. Serve immediately.

Serves 4–6

1/2 cup short-grain rice
4 cups milk
1 lemongrass stalk, bruised
1/2 cup superfine sugar
1 teaspoon vanilla extract
1 guava, sliced
1 small papaya, sliced

caramelized leek, goat cheese and spinach tart

Pastry
2 cups all-purpose flour
1/2 cup butter
3–4 tablespoons iced water

Filling
2 tablespoons olive oil
1 leek, thinly sliced
1 fennel bulb, thinly sliced
3 cups young spinach leaves
2 1/2 oz goat cheese,
crumbled
3 eggs, lightly beaten
2/3 cup whipping cream

Preheat the oven to 400°F. Place the flour and butter in a food processor and process until the mixture resembles bread crumbs. With the motor running, gradually add iced water until the pastry comes together. Gather into a ball, cover with plastic wrap and refrigerate for 20 minutes.

Roll the pastry out on a lightly floured surface to fit an 8 1/2-inch fluted tart pan. Ease into the pan and trim off excess pastry. Line with waxed paper and fill with baking weights or rice. Bake for 15 minutes, then remove the weights and the paper and bake for another 10 minutes. Reduce the oven temperature to 315°F.

Heat the oil in a frying pan, add the leek and fennel and cook over medium heat for 20 minutes or until the leeks are caramelized. Remove. Add the spinach and cook until it wilts. Spread the leek and fennel over the pastry shell and top with spinach and goat cheese. Combine the eggs and cream, pour into the pastry shell and bake for 40 minutes or until set.

Serves 6

Pandoro, a rich yellow yeast cake simliar to panettone, is eaten in Italy on festive occasions.

pandoro with poached peaches and mascarpone

Place the sugar, water, cardamom pods, bay leaf, vanilla and lemon juice in a large saucepan and stir over low heat until the sugar dissolves. Bring to a boil and add the peaches. Reduce the heat and simmer for 10 minutes. Remove the peaches, peel and halve. Boil the syrup until reduced by a third. Dip the pandoro or panettone into the combined egg and milk mixture. Heat the butter in a large frying pan and cook the pandoro or panettone in batches over medium heat until golden brown on both sides. Combine the mascarpone and brown sugar. Arrange the pandoro or panettone slices on plates, top with mascarpone and peaches and drizzle with the syrup. Garnish with a bay leaf.

Serves 4

1 cup sugar
4 cups water
3 cardamom pods, bruised
1 bay leaf
1 vanilla bean, split
juice of 1 lemon
6 peaches, pitted
4 small pandoro, cut into thick slices, or 1 small panettone, sliced
2 eggs, lightly beaten
2 cups milk
1/4 cup butter
3/4 cup mascarpone or sour cream
3 tablespoons brown sugar
fresh bay leaves, to garnish

Muesli—which in German means "mixture"—was invented in the late 19th century by Dr. Bircher-Benner.

healthy nut and seed muesli

1 cup puffed corn
1 1/2 cups rolled oats
1 cup pecans
1 cup macadamia nuts, roughly chopped
2 cups flaked coconut
6 1/2 oz linseed mix (linseed, sunflower seeds and almonds)
1 cup dried apples, chopped
1 cup dried apricots, chopped
1 cup dried pears, chopped
1/2 cup maple syrup
1 teaspoon vanilla extract

Preheat the oven to 350°F. Place the puffed corn, rolled oats, pecans, macadamia nuts, coconut, linseed mix, apples, apricots and pears in a bowl and mix to combine.

Place the maple syrup and vanilla in a small saucepan and cook over low heat for 3 minutes or until the maple syrup becomes easy to pour.

Pour maple syrup over the mixture and toss lightly to coat.

Divide the muesli mixture between 2 nonstick baking dishes. Bake for about 20 minutes, turning frequently, until the muesli is lightly toasted. Allow the mixture to cool before transferring it to an airtight container.

Makes 1 kg

Buttermilk is made by adding organisms and cultures to skim or low-fat milk to sour it.

cheese and herb corn bread with scrambled eggs

Preheat the oven to 350°F. Grease an 8 inch x 4 inch loaf pan. Sift the flour, sugar, baking powder and salt into a bowl. Add the cornmeal, cheese, herbs, eggs, buttermilk and oil and mix to combine. Spoon the mixture into the loaf pan and bake for 45 minutes or until a skewer comes out clean. Remove from the pan.

To make the scrambled eggs, whisk together the eggs and cream and season with salt and pepper. Pour the mixture into a nonstick frying pan and cook over low heat, stirring occasionally until the egg is just set. (The more you stir the eggs, the more scrambled they become.) Serve the scrambled eggs with slices of buttered corn bread. Sprinkle with basil leaves.

Serves 4

Corn bread
1 1/4 cups self-rising flour
1 tablespoon superfine sugar
2 teaspoons baking powder
1 teaspoon salt
3/4 cup fine cornmeal
1/2 cup grated Cheddar cheese
1/2 cup chopped fresh mixed herbs
   (chives, dill, parsley)
2 eggs
1 cup buttermilk
1/3 cup macadamia or olive oil

Scrambled eggs
6 eggs
1/2 cup whipping cream
salt and pepper
small basil leaves, to garnish

Capers have a slightly bitter flavor.
They are suited to seafood and
come pickled in a vinegar brine.

bagels with smoked salmon and caper salsa

4 plain or rye bagels
1/3 cup Philadelphia cream cheese
61/2 oz sliced smoked salmon
2 scallions, chopped
2 plum tomatoes, finely chopped
2 tablespoons baby capers
2 tablespoons finely chopped
fresh dill
2 tablespoons lemon juice
1 tablespoon extra-virgin olive oil

Cut the bagels in half and spread the
bottom generously with cream cheese,
then top with the salmon. Combine the
scallions, tomatoes, capers, dill, lemon
juice and olive oil in a bowl. Pile this
mixture onto the salmon and serve.

Serves 4

Whitebait is the name given
to the tiny transparent fry of the
herring family.

whitebait with crème fraîche tartare

Rinse the whitebait and pat dry. Place the flour in a bowl and season with salt and pepper. Toss the whitebait in the flour, shaking off any excess. Heat the oil in a deep frying pan until a cube of bread browns in 15 seconds when dropped into it. Cook the whitebait in batches until crisp and golden. This won't take very long— about 1 or 2 minutes. Remove and drain on paper towels.

To make the tartar sauce, combine the crème fraîche, mayonnaise, gherkins, capers, lemon juice and parsley in a bowl. Serve piles of the fried whitebait on plates, accompanied with a small bowl of tartar sauce.

Serves 4

1 lb whitebait, such as sand eel
   or silversides
1 cup all-purpose flour
salt and pepper
vegetable oil, for deep-frying

Tartar sauce
3/4 cup crème fraîche or
   sour cream
2 tablespoons whole egg mayonnaise
3 gherkins, finely chopped
2 tablespoons capers, finely chopped
1 teaspoon lemon juice
1 tablespoon chopped fresh
   flat-leaf parsley

Ratatouille, a type of vegetable casserole, is a popular dish from the region of Nice in France.

chunky ratatouille tarts

1 eggplant, cut into 1 1/4-inch cubes
1 red bell pepper, cut into 1 1/4-inch cubes
3 zucchini, cut into thick slices
1 red onion, chopped into large pieces
2 tablespoons olive oil
6 1/2 oz teardrop (pear) or cherry tomatoes
1 cup kalamata olives, pitted
2 tablespoons finely shredded basil
salt and pepper
2 sheets frozen puff pastry, thawed
1 egg, lightly beaten
shredded basil, extra, to garnish

Preheat the oven to 400°F. Sprinkle the eggplant with salt, let it rest for 15 minutes, then rinse and pat dry. Place the eggplant, bell pepper, zucchini and onions in a roasting pan, add the oil and toss to coat. Bake the vegetables for 40 minutes, tossing frequently. Add the tomatoes and bake for 5 minutes. Transfer all the vegetables to a bowl, stir in the kalamata olives and basil and season with salt and pepper. Strain the mixture to remove any juices.

Cut each pastry sheet into 4 squares and place on a baking sheet lined with waxed paper. Cut 16 3/4-inch wide strips to fit around the edges of each square. Divide the ratatouille among the squares. Brush the pastry edges with beaten egg and bake for 25 minutes or until golden. Garnish with basil.

Serves 4

Cilantro, also known as Chinese parsley, is reputed to act as an appetite stimulant.

thai chicken sausage rolls

Preheat the oven to 400°F. Combine the chicken, cumin, ground coriander, chili sauce, cilantro leaves and bread crumbs in a bowl. Spread the mixture along one edge of each pastry sheet and roll up to conceal the filling. Place the rolls seam side down on a baking sheet lined with waxed paper, brush lightly with the beaten egg and sprinkle with sesame seeds. Bake for 30 minutes or until golden and cooked through. Slice the rolls and serve with arugula and sweet chili sauce.

Serves 6–8

1 lb ground chicken
1 teaspoon ground cumin
1 teaspoon ground coriander
2 tablespoons sweet chili sauce
2 tablespoons chopped fresh
   cilantro leaves
1 cup fresh bread crumbs
2 sheets frozen puff pastry, thawed
1 egg, lightly beaten
1 tablespoon sesame seeds
baby arugula leaves, to serve
sweet chili sauce, extra, for dipping

You can use any edible flowers for this recipe. Baby roses or nasturtiums look very pretty.

champagne and blueberry jellies

3 teaspoons gelatin
1²/3 cups champagne
4 tablespoons superfine sugar
4 pansy or violet flowers
1/4 cup small blueberries

Place the gelatin, champagne and sugar in a saucepan. Stir over low heat until the gelatin dissolves, then simmer for 2 minutes. Allow to cool slightly while you lightly grease 4 1/2-cup molds and carefully place a pansy or violet in the center of each base (face-side of the flowers downwards). Pour enough of the champagne liquid over the flowers to just cover them. Refrigerate until set. Chill the remaining liquid.
Divide the berries amongst the molds and pour over the remaining champagne liquid. Refrigerate until set. To serve, use your fingers to release the jellies from their molds. If you have trouble getting them out, rub the outsides of the molds with a warm cloth to slightly melt the jelly.

Serves 4

Cinnamon is the aromatic inner bark of the evergreen cinnamon tree, which is indigenous to Sri Lanka.

cinnamon oatmeal with caramel figs and cream

Place the oats, water and cinnamon in a saucepan and stir over medium heat for 5 minutes until the oatmeal becomes thick and smooth. Set the oatmeal aside.

Melt the butter in a large frying pan, add all but 2 tablespoons of the brown sugar and stir until it dissolves. Stir in the cream and bring to a boil, then simmer for 5 minutes or until the sauce starts to thicken slightly.

Place the figs onto a baking sheet, sprinkle with the remaining sugar and broil until the sugar is melted.

Spoon the oatmeal into individual bowls, top with a little milk, then divide the figs and the caramel sauce among the bowls. Top each serving with a large dollop of heavy cream.

Serves 4

2 cups rolled oats
4 cups water
1/4 teaspoon ground cinnamon
2 tablespoons butter
1/2 cup brown sugar
11/4 cups whipping cream
6 fresh figs, halved
milk, to serve
1/3 cup heavy cream,
    to serve

Ready to eat in minutes, this colorful dish is a delicious way to start a summer's day.

mixed berry couscous

1 cup couscous
2 cups apple and cranberry juice
1 cinnamon stick
1 1/4 cups raspberries
1 cup blueberries
1 cup blackberries
1 cup strawberries, halved
zest of 1 lime, grated
zest of 1 orange, grated
2/3 cup yogurt
2 tablespoons golden or dark corn syrup
mint leaves, to garnish

Place the couscous in a bowl. Place the apple and cranberry juice in a saucepan with the cinnamon stick. Bring to a boil, then remove from the heat and pour over the couscous. Cover with plastic wrap and allow to rest for 5 minutes or until all the liquid has been absorbed. Remove and discard the cinnamon stick. Separate the grains of the couscous with a fork, add the raspberries, blueberries, blackberries, strawberries, lime zest and orange zest and fold in gently. Spoon the mixture into 4 bowls and serve with a generous dollop of yogurt and a drizzle of syrup. Garnish with mint leaves.

Serves 4

Jamaica and India produce
the majority of the world's
supply of ginger.

ginger and ricotta pancakes with fresh honeycomb

Sift the flour, baking powder, ginger and sugar into a bowl. Stir in the coconut and make a well in the center. Add the combined egg yolks, 1 1/2 cups of the ricotta and all of the milk. Mix until smooth. Beat the egg whites until soft peaks form, then fold into the pancake mixture. Heat a frying pan and brush lightly with a little melted butter or oil. Pour 1/4 cup of the batter into the pan and swirl gently to create an even pancake. Cook over low heat until bubbles form on the surface. Flip and cook the other side for 1 minute or until golden. Continue until all the batter is used up. Stack three pancakes onto each plate and top with a generous dollop of ricotta, sliced banana and a large piece of fresh honeycomb.

Serves 4

1 cup whole wheat flour
2 teaspoons baking powder
2 teaspoons ground ginger
2 tablespoons superfine sugar
1 cup coconut flakes, toasted
4 eggs, separated
2 cups ricotta
1 1/4 cups milk
4 bananas, sliced
1/2 cup fresh honeycomb, broken into large pieces, as a garnish

Store mushrooms in paper bags
in the refrigerator. If stored in
plastic, they tend to sweat.

crispy pita bread tiles with butter mushrooms

3 pieces pita bread or Arab flat bread
2 tablespoons olive oil
1/4 cup finely grated parmesan
cheese
1/3 cup butter
4 scallions, sliced
1 1/2 lb mixed mushrooms
(porcini, button, cremini,
Portobello, enoki), sliced
1 tablespoon chervil leaves

Preheat the oven to 350°F. Cut the pita bread or Arab flat bread into 1 1/4-inch wide strips and brush lightly with 1 tablespoon of the oil. Sprinkle with the grated parmesan cheese and bake for 10 minutes or until crisp. Heat the butter and the remaining oil in a large frying pan until sizzling. Add the scallions and the porcini mushrooms and cook over medium heat until the mushrooms are tender. Add the cremini mushrooms, Portobello and button mushrooms and cook until the liquid has evaporated. Remove from the heat and mix in the enoki mushrooms.
Arrange the toasted strips of bread into an interlocking square. Pile the mushrooms in the center, garnish with chervil and serve immediately.

Serves 4

Ricotta is a fresh cheese made from the whey that is drained off in the process of making mozzarella.

individual herbed lemon ricotta

Lightly grease and line 4 1/2-cup ramekins with plastic wrap. Divide the ricotta between the molds and press down firmly. Cover with plastic wrap and refrigerate for 2 hours. Preheat the oven to 425°F. Unmold the ricottas onto a baking sheet lined with waxed paper and bake for 20 minutes or until golden. To make the dressing, combine all the ingredients in a bowl. Place each baked ricotta into a shallow bowl and pour a little of the dressing over each one. Serve immediately with crusty fresh bread.

Serves 4

2 cups ricotta

Dressing
2 tablespoons olive oil
1 clove garlic, crushed
zest of 1 lemon
2 tablespoons lemon juice
1 tablespoon balsamic vinegar
1/2 cup olive oil
5 oz sun-dried tomatoes, roughly chopped
4 tablespoons chopped fresh parsley

crusty bread, to serve

twice-baked cheese soufflés

1 cup milk
3 black peppercorns
1 onion, cut in half and studded with
2 cloves
1 bay leaf
1/4 cup butter
1/4 cup self-rising flour
2 eggs, separated
1 cup gruyère cheese, grated
1 cup whipping cream
1/2 cup parmesan cheese,
finely grated

Preheat the oven to 350°F. Lightly grease 4 1/2-cup ramekins. Place the milk, peppercorns, onion and bay leaf in a saucepan and heat until nearly boiling. Remove from the heat and let infuse for 10 minutes. Strain.

Melt the butter in a saucepan, add the flour and cook over medium heat for 1 minute. Remove from the heat and gradually stir in the infused milk, then return to the heat and stir until the mixture boils and thickens. Simmer for 1 minute. Transfer the mixture to a bowl and add the egg yolks and gruyère cheese. Beat the egg whites until soft peaks form, then gently fold into the cheese sauce. Divide the mixture between the ramekins and place in a baking dish half-filled with hot water. Bake for 15 minutes. Remove from the baking dish, cool and refrigerate. Preheat the oven to 400°F, remove the soufflés from the ramekins and place onto flameproof plates. Pour cream over the top and sprinkle with parmesan. Bake for 20 minutes or until puffed and golden. Serve with a salad.

Serves 4

These can be made ahead of time and the uncooked rolls frozen. Thaw before baking.

choc-hazelnut puff pastry rolls

1/4 cup Nutella (chocolate-hazelnut spread)
2/3 cup confectioners' sugar
2 sheets frozen puff pastry, thawed
1 egg, lightly beaten
confectioners' sugar, to dust

Preheat the oven to 400°F. Combine the Nutella and confectioners' sugar and roll into an 8-inch long roll. Wrap the roll in plastic wrap and twist the ends to enclose. Refrigerate for 30 minutes. When firm, cut the roll into 8 even pieces. Roll each of the pieces in confectioners' sugar. Cut each sheet of puff pastry into 4 squares. Place a piece of the Nutella roll onto each square of pastry and roll up to enclose. Pinch the ends and brush lightly with egg. Bake for 15 minutes or until the pastry is golden. Dust with confectioners' sugar.

Serves 4

potato flowers with salmon, asparagus and quail eggs

Dressing
1/4 cup whole egg mayonnaise
2 tablespoons plain yogurt
2 cloves garlic, crushed
1 tablespoon lime juice

1/2 cup butter
4 medium potatoes, peeled and cut into paper-thin slices
salt
24 fresh asparagus spears
8 quail or regular eggs
6 1/2 oz gravlax or smoked salmon slices

Place all the dressing ingredients in a bowl and whisk to combine. Preheat the oven to 475°F. Melt the butter in a small saucepan, spoon off any froth that settles on top, and carefully pour off the yellow butter, discarding the milky sediment in the bottom of the pan. Pour half of the butter onto a baking sheet. Toss the potato slices in salt, then place 4 potato slices about 6 inches apart onto the baking sheet. These will be the centers of your flowers. Arrange the remaining slices around them, overlapping to form 8 flowers. Brush with a little more butter. Bake for 8 minutes or until the edges are brown, then turn and cook for another 3 minutes or until cooked through. Steam the asparagus spears until tender. Remelt the extra butter in a nonstick frying pan, crack the eggs using a small knife, and cook over low heat for 1–2 minutes or until the whites have set. Serve 2 potato flowers on each plate topped with the steamed asparagus, slices of gravlax or smoked salmon, 2 eggs and the mayonnaise dressing.

Serves 4

Sweet, oily pecan nuts belong to the hickory family and are native to the southern parts of the country.

pecan phyllo sheets with fried apples

Preheat the oven to 400°F. Brush 1 sheet of phyllo pastry with the melted butter. Top with another sheet, sprinkle with $1/3$ of the pecans and sugar, top with another layer of phyllo, brush with butter and repeat the layering and sprinkling until you have used all the pastry, pecans and sugar. Use scissors to cut the pastry in half, then cut each half into 8 triangles. Place the triangles on 2 baking sheets and bake for 10 minutes or until crisp and golden. Heat the extra butter in a large frying pan, add the spices and apples and cook over medium heat for 5 minutes, turning the apples once, until they are soft and golden. Serve accompanied with phyllo triangles and a spoonful of mascarpone. Dust with nutmeg.

Serves 4–6

8 sheets phyllo pastry
3 tablespoons butter, melted
1 cup pecans, chopped
$1/4$ cup brown sugar
$1/3$ cup butter, extra
$1/2$ teaspoon freshly grated nutmeg
1 teaspoon ground cinnamon
$1/4$ teaspoon ground cloves
4 small granny smith apples, sliced into $1/2$-inch thick slices horizontally (do not peel or core)
$6^{1}/2$ oz mascarpone
extra nutmeg, for dusting

Asparagus is the young, edible
shoot of a leafless plant that is
a member of the lily family.

char-grilled asparagus with salsa

3 eggs
2 tablespoons milk
1 tablespoon olive oil
2 cobs corn
1 small red onion, diced
1 red bell pepper, finely
chopped
2 tablespoons chopped fresh thyme
2 tablespoons olive oil, extra
2 tablespoons balsamic vinegar
24 fresh asparagus spears
1 tablespoon macadamia or olive oil
toasted whole grain bread, to serve

Beat the eggs and milk to combine.
Heat the oil in a nonstick frying pan,
add the egg and cook over medium
heat until just set. Flip and cook the
other side. Remove and allow to cool,
then roll up and cut into thick slices.
Cook the corn on a grill or in boiling
water until tender. Set aside to cool
slightly, then slice off the corn kernels.
Make the salsa by gently combining the
corn, onions, bell pepper, thyme,
olive oil and balsamic vinegar.
Trim off any woody ends from the
asparagus, lightly brush with macadamia
or olive oil and cook on the grill until
tender. Serve the asparagus topped
with a little salsa and the finely
shredded egg, accompanied by fingers
of buttered, toasted whole grain bread.

Serves 4–6

The vanilla bean was once highly prized as an aphrodisiac and was the preserve of royalty.

star anise, lime and vanilla tropical fruit salad

Place the watermelon, pineapple, mangoes, guava, papaya, litchis and kiwi fruit in a bowl and gently combine. Place the lime juice, palm sugar, star anise, vanilla bean, lime zest and water in a saucepan and stir over low heat until the sugar dissolves. Bring to a boil, reduce the heat and simmer for 10 minutes or until the syrup is reduced by half. Allow to cool slightly. Pour the syrup over the fruit and refrigerate until cold.

Serves 6

2 lb watermelon, cut into large pieces
1 small pineapple, peeled and chopped
2 mangoes, sliced
1 guava, sliced
1 small papaya, cut into large pieces
12 litchis, peeled
3 kiwi fruit, sliced
1/4 cup lime juice
3/4 cup grated palm sugar or brown sugar
6 star anise seeds
1 vanilla bean, split in half
zest of 1 lime, cut in thin strips
1 cup water

Field mushrooms, or Portobello mushrooms, can grow as large as 6 inches in diameter.

mushrooms with marinated feta

2 large tomatoes
20 fresh asparagus spears
10 oz marinated feta
1/4 cup extra-virgin olive oil
zest of 1 lemon, cut in thin strips
2 cloves garlic, crushed
2 tablespoons lemon juice
cracked black pepper
4 large Portobello mushrooms, brushed clean and stems removed
4 eggs
fresh oregano, to garnish

Cut the tomatoes into thick slices. Trim the ends from the asparagus. Drain the oil from the feta and place into a nonmetallic bowl. Stir in the olive oil, lemon zest, garlic and lemon juice. Season with pepper.

Place the mushrooms and tomatoes in a shallow dish and pour the oil mixture over them. Toss gently to coat, and marinate for 15 minutes. Drain the mushrooms, reserving the marinade, and cook them, together with the tomatoes, on a lightly oiled barbecue grill until tender. Add the asparagus towards the end of cooking, and lastly the eggs. Place the mushrooms on a plate, top each one with the asparagus spears, a slice of tomato, an egg and some sliced feta. Drizzle with the oil marinade and garnish with oregano.

Serves 4

Rose water, a tincture of rose oil and distilled water, is widely used in Middle Eastern cooking.

pancakes with rose water strawberries and butter

Sift the flour, baking powder, sugar and salt into a bowl and make a well in the center. Mix together the eggs, milk and butter in a bowl and pour into the well. Whisk to form a smooth batter. Cover and allow to rest for 20 minutes. Heat a nonstick frying pan and brush with extra melted butter. Pour 1/4 cup of batter into the pan and swirl gently. Cook over low heat for 1 minute or until bubbles burst on the surface.

Turn the pancake over and cook the other side. Transfer to a plate and keep warm while cooking the remaining batter. Combine the sugar and cinnamon and toss each pancake in the mixture. Combine the strawberries, rose water, vanilla and maple syrup. Serve stacks of the pancakes topped with whipped butter and the strawberry mixture.

1 1/2 cups self-rising flour
1 teaspoon baking powder
2 tablespoons superfine sugar
pinch salt
2 eggs, lightly beaten
1 cup milk
1/4 cup butter, melted
extra melted butter
1 cup superfine sugar, extra
1 tablespoon ground cinnamon
2 2/3 cups strawberries, halved
2 teaspoons rose water (optional)
1 teaspoon vanilla extract
1/4 cup maple syrup
1/3 cup butter, softened
   and whipped

Serves 4

The coffee bean is thought to have travelled from Ethiopia to Brazil and Colombia, today's big producers.

high-top cappuccino and white-choc muffins

1/4 cup instant espresso coffee powder
1 tablespoon boiling water
21/2 cups self-rising flour
1/2 cup superfine sugar
2 eggs, lightly beaten
11/2 cups buttermilk
1 teaspoon vanilla extract
2/3 cup butter melted
31/2 oz white chocolate, roughly chopped
2 tablespoons butter, extra
3 tablespoons brown sugar

Preheat the oven to 400°F. Cut 8 lengths of waxed paper and roll into 3-inch high cylinders to fit into 8 1/2-cup ramekins. When in place in the ramekins, secure the cylinders with string and place all the ramekins onto a baking sheet. Dissolve the coffee in boiling water and allow to cool. Sift the flour and sugar into a bowl. Combine the eggs, buttermilk, vanilla, melted butter, white chocolate and the coffee mixture and mix roughly with the dry ingredients. Spoon the mixture into each cylinder. Heat the extra butter and brown sugar and stir until the sugar dissolves. Spoon this mixture onto each muffin and gently swirl into the muffin using a skewer. Bake for 25–30 minutes or until risen and cooked when tested with a skewer.

Makes 8